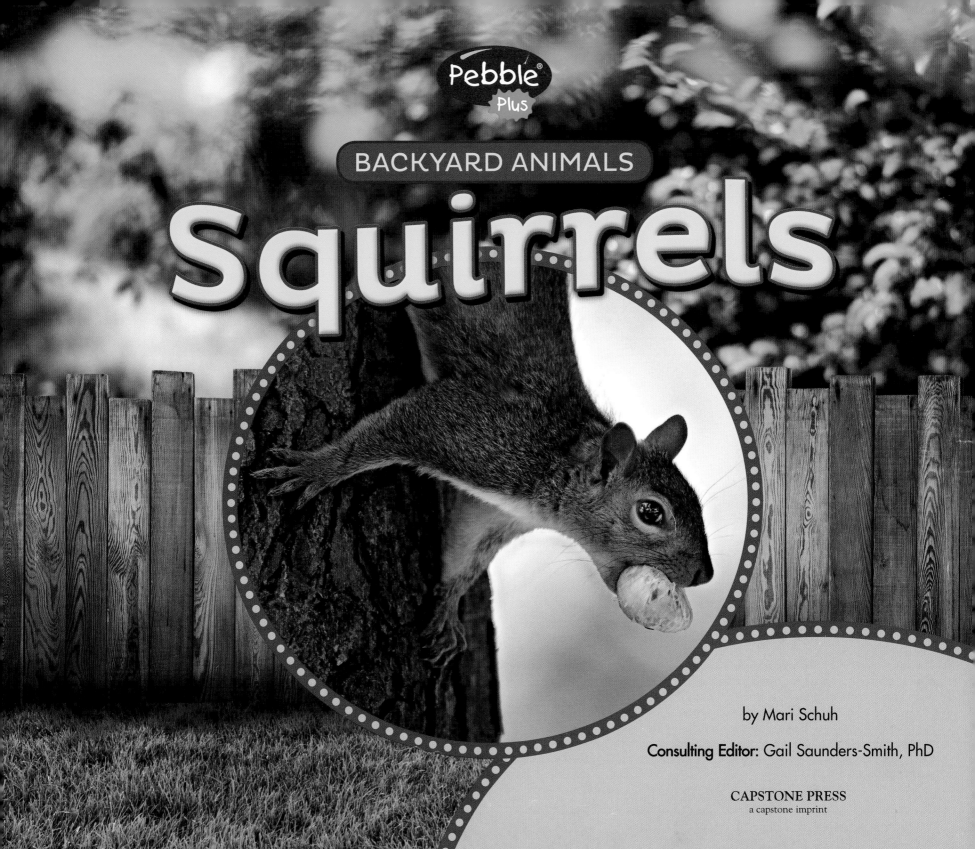

Pebble® Plus

BACKYARD ANIMALS

Squirrels

by Mari Schuh

Consulting Editor: Gail Saunders-Smith, PhD

CAPSTONE PRESS
a capstone imprint

Pebble Plus is published by Capstone Press,
1710 Roe Crest Drive, North Mankato, Minnesota 56003
www.capstonepub.com

Library of Congress Cataloging-in-Publication Data
Schuh, Mari C., 1975– author.
  Squirrels / by Mari Schuh.
pages cm. — (Pebble plus. Backyard animals)
Summary: "An introduction to squirrels, their characteristics, habitat, food, life cycle,
and threats. Includes a hands-on activity related to wildlife watching"— Provided by
publisher.
  Audience: Ages 4–8.
  Audience: K to grade 3.
  Includes bibliographical references and index.
ISBN 978-1-4914-2088-1 (library binding) — ISBN 978-1-4914-2329-5 (ebook PDF)
  1. Squirrels—Juvenile literature. I. Title.
QL737.R68S3487 2015
599.36—dc23   2014032329

Editorial Credits
Nikki Bruno Clapper, editor; Juliette Peters, designer;
Tracy Cummins, media researcher; Tori Abraham, production specialist

Photo Credits
Dreamstime: Alian226, 22 (hickory nut), Altair87, 22 (Black walnut); Shutterstock: Agustin
Esmoris, 1, Baloncici, 5, Hurst Photo, 22 (acorn), ILYA AKINSHIN, 21, Julija Sapic, 17
Background, 7 Background, Kellis, 11, Luka Balkovic, 13, Mark Caunt, Cover, Matin, 22
(chestnut), MVPhoto, 24, Nagel Photography, 7, Pagina, Back Cover, PinkPueblo, Design
Element, Svetlana Foote, 22 (squirrel), Varuna, 2, 23, 25, 1, Cover (fence), Welcomia, 9;
SuperStock: Minden Pictures, 17; Thinkstock: CCCollins, 19, Jim Sorrels, 15.

Note to Parents and Teachers

The Backyard Animals set supports national curriculum standards for science related
to life science and ecosystems. This book describes and illustrates squirrels. The
images support early readers in understanding the text. The repetition of words and
phrases helps early readers learn new words. This book also introduces early readers
to subject-specific vocabulary words, which are defined in the Glossary section. Early
readers may need assistance to read some words and to use the Table of Contents,
Glossary, Read More, Internet Sites, Critical Thinking Using the Common Core, and
Index sections of the book.

Printed in the United States of America in Stevens Point, Wisconsin.
092014   008479WZS15

Table of Contents

Backyard Squirrels

A long, bushy tail pops up from behind a fence. A furry animal jumps to a fence post and sniffs the air. There is a squirrel in your backyard!

Squirrels are rodents.
Their sharp teeth never
stop growing. Most squirrels
weigh less than 3 pounds
(1.4 kilograms).

A squirrel's big tail helps it balance. Sharp claws help the squirrel hold on tight as it climbs trees.

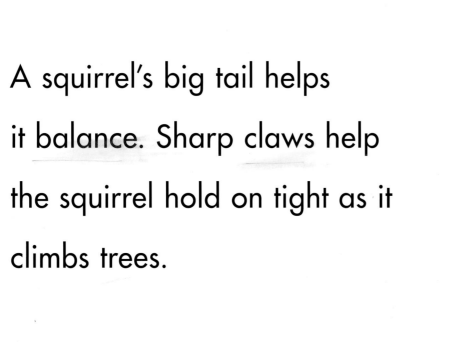

Squirrels live on every continent except Australia and Antarctica. Some squirrels make nests in trees. Others dig burrows.

What Squirrels Do

Squirrels spend a lot of time looking for food. They eat nuts, seeds, fruit, pinecones, and insects. Squirrels bury food to eat in the winter.

Squirrels are very fast.

They can run 20 miles

(32 kilometers) per hour.

They dart back and forth

to confuse predators.

Female squirrels give birth to two to eight babies at a time. Baby squirrels are hairless at birth. They grow fur within a few weeks.

Young squirrels stay
with their mother for two to
three months. Then they live
on their own. Most squirrels
live for about five years.

Feeding Time

You can give squirrels a special feeder in your yard. Fill it with sunflower seeds and nuts. Then watch your furry friends!

Hands-On Activity: **Nut Hunt**

Squirrels eat all kinds of nuts. Look at the pictures below. See if you can find some of these nuts in your backyard or neighborhood. An adult can help you.

acorn **chestnut** **hickory nut** **walnut**

Glossary

balance—to keep steady and not fall over

burrow—a hole or tunnel in the ground made or used by an animal

continent—one of earth's seven large land masses

predator—an animal that hunts other animals for food

rodent—a mammal with long front teeth used for gnawing; chipmunks, squirrels, rats, and beavers are rodents

Read More

Appleby, Alex. *I See a Squirrel.* In My Backyard. New York: Gareth Stevens Pub., 2013.

Lundgren, Julie K. *Squirrels.* Life Cycles. Vero Beach, Fla.: Rourke Pub., 2011.

Roza, Greg. *Your Neighbor the Squirrel.* City Critters. New York: Windmill Books, 2012.

Internet Sites

FactHound offers a safe, fun way to find Internet sites related to this book. All of the sites on FactHound have been researched by our staff.

Here's all you do:

Visit *www.facthound.com*

Type in this code: 9781491420881

 Check out projects, games and lots more at **www.capstonekids.com**

Critical Thinking
Using the Common Core

1. What do squirrels eat? (Key Ideas and Details)

2. Look at the pictures. Why do you think squirrels spend time in people's backyards? (Integration of Knowledge and Ideas)

Index

Word Count: 201
Grade: 1
Early-Intervention Level: 18